From Chaos to Order - 14 Days of Advanced Decluttering

Mari Sellin

Published by Mari Sellin, 2024.

Table of Contents

To Bo!

Thank you for being here!

MARI SELLIN

From Chaos to Order

14 Days of Advanced Decluttering

First published by Admiranda Publishing 2024

Copyright © 2024 by Mari Sellin

All rights reserved. No part of this publication may be reproduced, stored or transmitted in any form or by any means, electronic, mechanical, photocopying, recording, scanning, or otherwise without written permission from the publisher. It is illegal to copy this book, post it to a website, or distribute it by any other means without permission.

Mari Sellin asserts the moral right to be identified as the author of this work.

Mari Sellin has no responsibility for the persistence or accuracy of URLs for external or third-party Internet Websites referred to in this publication and does not guarantee that any content on such Websites is, or will remain, accurate or appropriate.

Designations used by companies to distinguish their products are often claimed as trademarks. All brand names and product names used in this book and on its cover are trade names, service marks, trademarks and registered trademarks of their respective owners. The publishers and the book are not associated with any product or vendor mentioned in this book. None of the companies referenced within the book have endorsed the book.

First edition

ISBN (print): 978-91-988625-7-7

ISBN (kindle): 978-91-988625-5-3

ISBN (eBook): 978-91-988625-4-6

Second edition

ISBN (print): 979-82-306468-8-4

Introduction

Welcome to From Chaos to Order – 14 Days of Advanced Decluttering. A crash course in how to help yourself tidy up your home, a friend's house, or perhaps someone's estate. Good planning enables you to reach your goal faster.

My name is Mari Sellin, and I am very excited to share this knowledge with you. It's the best way I can do it to help more people get their homes, houses, and other living areas in order. For several years, I have enjoyed helping people get their homes in order, giving them a more peaceful home and sometimes even a new lifestyle.

To help people with an average amount of stuff in their smaller homes, I've written a crash course on how they help themselves in two days (see the book "Weekend Decluttering - From Chaos to Calm in 48 Hours for Home Harmony and Inner Peace").

However, there are bigger houses with more than three rooms and a kitchen. Some people have accumulated so many things that they have taken over the home. Instead of living in their own homes and having items placed in their rooms, the apartment or house is a warehouse with things and has a person/people staying in selected parts of the space.

This book is for those who realize their challenge is a project requiring more than two days to solve. But I want to give you hope. As long as you have prepared well and, in the case of having a lot of things, enlisted the help of family and friends or external labor, you can declutter a larger home or empty it in two weeks. Because you have prepared well, you can supervise yourself and others in your decluttering project. It saves time and speeds up the whole process.

In the chapter Different Reasons and Degrees of Misery, you will find a brief description with examples of the most common types of collectors I have encountered. These descriptions can help you quickly understand that you are like many others or that there are people with a greater need for decluttering.

The intention is to help everyone understand that many people can have small or large collecting behaviors without perhaps realizing that this is the case. Based on that knowledge, you better understand yourself or someone else. Maybe even see the opportunity to get to know each other better while actively cleaning up the situation together.

It sometimes happens that instead of tackling the decluttering need, people start thinking about buying new storage boxes or new, better-adapted furniture to house their things or even plan to rent a storage room. Wait until after you've completed your decluttering. Afterward, the need for new things may become unnecessary. First, we declutter, and then we see if there is a lack of a suitable place to store things.

The same applies if you want to decorate according to, for example, Feng shui. Declutter first, and you might find an item you already have that you like and can use.

This book assumes that there may be three root causes for your need to read this book about decluttering.

- A person or family with too much stuff needs decluttering and getting organized.

- A person or persons who realizes that a friend or relative has a hoarding problem and needs help but wonders what and how to do it.

- People who inherit a collector's property need help doing a death-cleaning.

The chapters where I need to highlight something extra concerning the situation where you help someone else or manage the household of a large collector provide more specific information.

Of course, the time required depends on the size of your home and how many people are there to help you. But even if you are alone and have a lot of things, you have time to declutter a bigger home in two weeks. Even cleaning, even if it is a premium in this context.

The only thing you need to do is decide to declutter. Read through chapters four through six (when, what order, what things, and how) in this book, decide which weeks to do it, and prepare well.

The chapters show how I think when I work on decluttering. If you suddenly feel unmotivated, jump into chapter two to find reasons to continue. If you believe you have more significant problems than others, read chapter three and realize that that thought is not valid or that you are at least not alone. Take one thing at a time!

Why is a Decluttering Needed?

Image 1. A clean house reflects a clear mind and a peaceful heart.

This book assumes that there may be three root causes for decluttering.

- A person or family with too much stuff needs decluttering and getting organized.

- A person or persons who realizes that a friend or relative has a hoarding problem and needs help but wonders what and how to do it.

- People who inherit a collector's property need help with how to start.

Things matter!

Understanding what follows below in this chapter can increase motivation. It increases the understanding that the things you surround yourself with affect your feelings. But they can also affect future events and other people. Decluttering can help people understand why they buy things and what they want.

It may not help those who have inherited a "hoarding problem." In the case of inherited "things," it doesn't matter. Someone has to do it no matter what. But to avoid inheriting the problem, maybe you can find motivating factors you can take with your relative or friend. That way, you can handle the situation while the owner is still alive.

Emotionally

Being satisfied and comfortable with your accommodation helps you feel good. If you have lived in overcrowded rooms, you will find more freedom, peace, calm, and joy after decluttering your home. Being messy or overcrowded with things unknowingly stresses you out.

Decluttering can give you, or if you help someone else, a fresh start in life. Out with the old things that have slowed down the energy in your home and your life. In with fresh air and space for you to be and live in.

Some are ashamed of their situation. They may not even want to invite someone home. Have you never been invited to the home of someone you think is close to you? You might have someone there who would appreciate your help!

Some don't go to work for a couple of days or a week because they feel they need to declutter and clean before a dinner party with friends or relatives. Cleaning only occurs in the rooms where the guests are allowed to go. Things end up in the other rooms where the doors are closed for guests to visit.

Better Short-term Finances

As times change, so does fashion. You can find things you don't want to keep but can sell as demand increases. With increased demand, the item you have may be worth more to you sold than stored. Think of, for example, Nintendo and LPs. New variants have arrived. But the demand for the old has increased in parts of the world. So, if you take your time, decluttering can also provide better short-term finances. If you find a buyer who wants what you have at home and no longer wishes to keep yourself.

Better Long-term Finances

Finding what you're looking for will help you have a healthier economy. The risk increases that you go and buy a new copy completely unnecessarily just because you couldn't find what you were looking for.

The financial aspect might feel a little silly, but the fact is that your decluttering can help you have a better economy in the long run. While cleaning your home, consider why you bought the various things. By figuring out why, you become more aware and can create a change that will most likely help you get a better economy in the long run.

If you know why you buy things and ask yourself if you need them, you can consciously start making better financial choices. Instead, investing or saving a smaller amount of money each month may feel boring now, but it will make you grateful later on. (Ensure you take help or invest through certified and safe services to avoid scamming.)

An easy budget-example

Below is one method that most of my customers appreciated and liked to use when creating an overview of their finances. It was initially designed to help clients understand what income they could use for various expenses and to clarify how credit card use works.

One of the easiest ways to create and keep a budget is as follows:

Take out at least two sheets of paper (or write on the front and back) and draw two vertical lines from top to bottom to have three columns on each page.

Column 1: In the leftmost column, write the first six months of the year (January to June) on one sheet, and the last six months (July to December) are entered on the other sheet. (If you want to write large or need many lines per month, you may need to write three months per page.)

Enter what you know in advance or can estimate in column 2 for each month:

Column 2 Plus items: Enter the income that you know for sure that you will receive each month.

Column 2 Minus items: Enter the costs for the house and vehicle. If you don't know, check last year's bank statement, and you'll know roughly when certain expenses will come and roughly what they cost last year. For example:

- Housing costs such as rent or amortization and interest.

- Costs for accommodation include insurance, electricity, heating, gas, and water.

- Top up with other existing loan costs.

- Top up with insurance.

- Also, enter any sums saved.

Column 2: Add up what's left after your relatively fixed monthly expenses reduce your income.

Now, over to the far right column. Here, you fill in additional costs during the current month.

Column 3 Plus item: Enter the amount left over from the month's column 2.

Column 3 Minus item: Enter your expenses:

- From the grocery store (food, toilet paper, soap).

- Fuel costs or costs for public transport.

- Enter any credit card amounts you must pay after last month's purchases. Start by writing down the amount you need for these costs with a pencil. Change when you know what happened.

The positive amount of money you have left in the last column is what you have left to spend on things and pleasures. Or save and invest.

If you have no money left, you need to question your expenses. It would be best to buy less or cheaper or generate more income.

Healthy Living

Image 2. A clean house isn't just for appearances; it's a healthy way of living.

If your home is easy to clean, you are also more likely to clean it.

When does it become unhealthy? If you have problems with vermin, such as bedbugs in the bedroom and living room, cockroaches running around at night, clothes moths in the wardrobe, and mealworms in the pantry, it may be easy to realize that something is incorrect.

I will return to the vermin problem, but I want to point out that if you have a problem with bed bugs or cockroaches, you must deal with them first. If you give away clothes or furniture with these problems, you are responsible for allowing them to spread and make someone else's life miserable.

Having mice running in the house walls and the attic can cause unwanted problems. If the electrical panel is recessed into the wall, the hole penetrations are leaky, and the wall construction allows the mice to get in, there is a risk that they will get into the electrical panel. In good cases, it will only be a power outage. In the worst case, you get phase problems if the old rocker switches break. If you have problems getting hold of the mice, see tips under chapter four, Time to Plan When the Decluttering will Take Place.

Safe Home Environment

Moving around the home without tripping over things on the floor is a safety issue. In an emergency, you and those staying in your home need to be able to evacuate quickly and safely. **Doors** must be opened easily and completely so that they do not prevent you from getting out or the emergency services (for example, firefighters and paramedics) from getting in and out.

The same applies to the **windows** if someone needs to use them to escape. Moving flower pots or some books is OK.

Safe **picture hanging** belongs to the premium course. Depending on the number of paintings, it may be best to set aside a few hours to review them and ensure the hanging is secure. These are primarily lighter paintings that have been mounted and suspended with string. The string becomes brittle over time, which can result in the painting eventually falling. The simplest solution is to replace the string with steel wire. If the painting falls, the painting motif or the expensive frame may break. Or that what is placed under and in front of the painting. In the worst case, it falls on a person or a pet.

Even **replanting** pots end up at a premium. If you have an unstable pot or, for example, an Aloe Vera that has grown larger than the pot can handle, the plant must be replanted into a heavier pot if you intend to keep it. Unfortunately, at least one person on our planet got an Aloe Vera on their head (and survived).

More Efficient and Time-Saving

The fact that things are in their designated places and you reach them saves time. You avoid frustration and stress. For example, on an occasion when you are looking for something you need to have with you but have little time before you need to run to the bus or need to jump into the car to make it to that meeting on time.

Improvement in Case of Disease-Related Cause

There may be an illness-related cause that is the root cause of the problem, for example, depression. Getting help to clean their home can help the affected person feel better. Decluttering the home can help the person feel that the burdensome problem is being thrown out simultaneously.

Different Reasons and Degrees of Misery

Image 3. "It's so full it's impossible to clean!" – Bo Ahlner

Only You?

Having to declutter your own home may sound simple. You can decide everything yourself. But there may be situations that, as embarrassing as it may feel, needing an assistant can help you move forward faster and achieve your goal more efficiently. You are probably the one who was responsible for the need for decluttering from the very beginning. Then, a helping hand may be what you need to succeed.

But why not try it yourself first? I know you can. Everyone can do it themselves as long as they desire to succeed. But if you know you probably won't be able to do it yourself, you must ask for help.

If you want help, ask someone in your family or a close and good friend who you think knows about the situation and does not judge you but, out of love for you, actually wants to help you. Likely, family members and friends who know your situation out of sensitivity, fear of conflict, or fear of hurting you have not dared to talk to you about the problem. That doesn't mean they don't want to help. They are waiting for you to say that you now recognize the need and want their help. Lend them this book to read through first, and they will understand the plan. Or talk through how you plan to do it.

Household of at Least Two People

Being more people in a household requires a mutual decision to participate. It would be best to do it together to motivate yourself to keep up with the new decided level. Decluttering together ensures that one person does not throw anything that has affective value to the other person.

If there are children in the family, it is good if they can participate and help. Talk about having a decluttering journey and explain what you plan to do. Listen and answer the children's questions. Children who are three years of age or older can usually help. If they are over eight years old, they should be able to clean their room based on your guidelines. If they are teenagers, they should be involved in the family's decluttering project. It will help them to learn how to think about things and money for the future. You show them that this is the new normal.

To Help Another Person

Is it the case that you have a close relative or friend you realize needs help with decluttering? Few people would probably appreciate it if you showed up with boxes and garbage bags one day and told them their home needs decluttering. Start by talking to them more sensitively. There is always an underlying reason why things turned out the way they did. Most people consciously or unconsciously realize that they may have a problem but don't know how to address it.

Ask if you can help and tell them about this book. Asking if the person wants to read this (or any other) book on decluttering rarely helps. It will probably just be a way to postpone a decision and get you to stop nagging for the moment. Then, it is better to tell them how you can lend a helping hand if only they want to accept the help and be involved.

The person you want to help must be "willing to receive help." The idea is NOT for you to declutter (or clean) someone else's home. Then, you are doing yourself and the other person a disservice. The idea is to do the essential work together, where you are involved and help steer the work forward. The person can then have you as help to avoid getting into trouble again by reminding, if necessary.

Death-cleaning

The concepts derive from emptying the home and other spaces of a deceased relative or an inherited person. You "inherit" someone else clutter. If you have a relative with a clutter problem, the tip is to try to get help from your affected heirs to help the relative get a grip on the situation jointly. If the relative does not care for it while there is time, the problem will end for you, who inherits.

It's one thing to inherit a well-maintained home where you only need to empty an average amount of furniture. It's quite another thing to inherit rooms filled with things. By that, I mean from floor to ceiling. At worst, it's rubbish where you have labyrinth passages wide enough to walk into the rooms.

Examples of Collector-Types

Below is a brief description, with descriptive examples, of the most common variants I have encountered to keep different types of collectors apart. Some have combined two or three of these types. They are listed so that you can see and understand differences.

Judge no one. It is essential to understand that many people have some form of hoarding behavior. That's how humans are. Aware of our collecting behavior, we can start to think before we shop and act in the future.

For those of you who want to help someone else, it is essential to realize that everyone has different interests and different degrees of involvement in their interest. When it gets out of hand, it can have negative consequences.

* * *

First, there are four types of collectors who see their clutter as something that approaches the feeling of Feng Shui or as a fortune. These people have a purpose for their collection, which joys them when they see their collectibles. These people probably do not see their things as "clutter" at all.

Treasure Keeper – A person who initially "just" wanted to save a few copies of something but then continued.

For example, collecting a few glass jars or plastic boxes to store leftovers, use as lunch boxes, or make jams and juices at home. The problem arose when saving behavior did not stop when the first shelf in the cabinet was full.

Cherish Collector – A person interested in more minor things who experiences their things more as ornaments. These things can be anything from tomato plants to angels, paintings, canvases, jewelry, clothes, shoes, electronics, axes, saws, and swords. They can function as investments, where they are sold and bought.

Thanks to Cherish Collectors, objects that later end up in museums or become collectibles sold at auctions are cared for and saved.

Relic Keeper – A collector with an interest in larger objects. Experience the things as ornaments, but the collection takes up more space. It could be furniture, sewing machines, cars, motorcycles, airplanes, horse-drawn carriages, engines, sawmills, or anything relatively large.

Most often, Relic Keepers start museums. They want a place to store their items properly, display them, and earn maintenance money. They're also popular entries at markets, shows, or other times where their items can be displayed to the public.

Picture 1. Does anyone else have a motorcycle in the living room?

Passion Purchaser – Creative person who wants to try new things and buys everything at once. Buy more than they have time to use it. It becomes a bad financial deal if the abundance is sold cheaper than the purchase price or given away when they discover they did not get attached to the interest.

I am, among other things, a Passion Purchaser. A descriptive example is when I started painting pictures and couldn't decide whether they should be in oil, acrylic, watercolor, or gouache. So, I should just as well buy paint, brushes, canvases, and sketchpads for all four, right? All four have advantages and disadvantages depending on the occasion, motive, and situation. But all things need to be stored and take up space.

* * *

Below are variants who may not be fully aware of their problem, ashamed of their situation, or hoping that someone could help them.

Chaos Creator – A person who tries to get rid of things. The things have already been packed, but before the box is stored or thrown away, it must be gone through "one last" time. The carton is turned upside down.

The feeling that it suddenly becomes too much overwhelms the person, who hopefully puts things back in the box and leaves it for later. In the worst case, things will remain where they ended up until the person decides that the situation must be dealt with. Suddenly, the cleaning ends in greater chaos than before.

Clutter Cleaner – A person who doesn't want or can't bear to get rid of things but still wants the home to be clean. Instead of questioning things, the objects are lifted regularly for cleaning on the surface underneath or of the object itself. The person cleans rather than starting to get rid of things.

Often, the difficulty of separating from things is based on fear—thoughts and beliefs that one must not separate from things and that one would be terrible if one did.

It could be because the things were always there. After all, they belonged to the deceased spouse or were gifts from someone. That the things somehow retain the memory of the loved one. Giving away can feel like they want to eliminate the one they loved. Busy thoughts that give negative feelings. So it's easier to keep things.

Wallet Waster – A person who has not learned to understand the value of money. They haven't learned how to make a monthly budget. They do not ensure that the income covers all monthly expenses BEFORE extraordinary or directly unnecessary purchases are made. They have difficulty keeping their money. As soon as the income comes, they buy things or use credit cards, which creates a negative spiral.

Credit cards involve the risk of interest. Everything bought may cost more than what was on the price tag at the time of purchase. Credit cards mean the user borrows money from someone else and postpones his payment for the item. "Someone else" is, for example, a bank or a company that usually requests interest on the borrowed money. Some give zero percent interest, for example, for the first 30 days. Most credit cards have a high interest rate. Credit cards are only a good solution for emergencies such as unexpected veterinary expenses or car repairs.

If you have financial problems, remember to ask for help. There is always a solution. It is just a matter of finding it.

Unfortunately, my experience is that not everyone has learned to understand what a "credit card" means. "It's my money," my client replied when I discovered that the fat wallet contained 20 credit cards! A more extended discussion ended with me being responsible for helping the person out of his credit card problem. Every month, he had to take out a few hundred of three cards to pay the interest on the others. To do the opposite next month. What saved the situation the most was that we sold his car. The money received became a monthly budget for food for two years, while the pension income went to rent, electricity, mobile phone, and installments. All other expenses were considered non-vital and removed. Thanks to a relatively high pension, the person became debt-free after 3,5 years. In addition, the person learned to stop using credit cards and have a much better relationship with money.

* * *

Now, there is an increasing risk that the labyrinth passages mentioned earlier will start to appear. It becomes challenging to reach furniture besides the furniture to which there are aisles. The most common maze targets are beds, toilets, kitchens, and sofas or armchairs with a view of the TV. You may walk on the floor but can also walk on things like newspapers and clothes—or worse.

Treasure Believer – A person who finds it difficult to throw, give away, or get rid of whole, well-functioning, and good-looking things. Sometimes, they believe the thing has value if they find the right buyer. However, to find the right buyer, one must take action, such as searching for a buyer or advertising, which is likely not prioritized. Another reason could be that the person doesn't want someone else to own the thing, only the person themselves.

Several decades ago, a company sold sports books in a subscription series. New books were published and sold yearly with the results of the country's and the world's largest competitions in athletics, football, ice hockey, etc. Different sports had their book. I remember it as if there were at least seven to ten different book topics. The seller had sold these books, saying that although they cost $100 each, when the buyer retired, they would be worth $3,000 each. When I came to their house, I found an entire basement room filled with several decades of books. Of the more than 200 books, at least twenty were not unpacked. In the owner's mind, they were retirement insurance. In reality, I could go into thrift stores and see how similar books were sold for $2 each.

Tidy Traumatized – A person almost constantly weighed down by thoughts about needing to clean. It feels like there are so many things that knowing where to start is hard. So it will be a big step to start.

As my client and I worked our way room by room on his Declutter Weekend, the person finally got to the root cause of the problem in the first place. Mother's nagging about cleaning the room! He had felt it like a punishment. Given that the person was now ashamed of their situation, it would not surprise me that the original situation in younger years had not been considered serious at all.

But we all do our best, even our parents. It becomes tough if we have to think about how everyone can be negatively affected by things we say. We cannot be responsible for how others choose to interpret the words we speak. It won't be easy to correct what was said or clarify one's intention if the other party does not tell us how they understood what we said. Or if we don't understand or perceive what the other party tries to explain.

We do not immediately understand when someone else's words harm us. Therefore, we rarely defend ourselves or ask the person to clarify.

Thinking about why you do things when you get older can be beneficial. The memories evoked may not always be pleasant. However, it can help us realize that our thoughts and conclusions when we were younger may not have been right. Based on your life experience, you may come to a more nuanced conclusion today.

Dust Dodger – A person who does not prioritize or have the energy to clean. Some make a conscious choice, but the most common is that there is a root cause in, for example, depression or brain fatigue/exhaustion symptoms. It is a sign that the person is crying out for help to deal with another more significant problem.

I have come across people who lack some mineral or vitamin in their body, are out in the sunlight too little, or don't like work and, therefore, become depressed.

When I was younger, I met a man who prioritized his animals in the barn. He only removed his shoes when he went to bed; otherwise, the barn clothes were on regularly. He was said to shower/bathe a few times a year before playing in the annual market. There was a disgusting smell of cattle and other things in his house, but the barn smelled fresh and clean. And the milk was award-winning.

Garbage Ghost – A person who, for psychological reasons, does not want to go out with their rubbish. It causes the garbage to be stored in piles in the home. People living alone in large houses can fill rooms with, for example, newspapers, packaging and rubbish.

I lived in a student corridor and was part of the tenants' association when I studied. At one meeting, the committed law student member did not show up. In connection with his visit to install fire alarms in each apartment, the landlord had to give the tenant an ultimatum. The tenant had been given a week, with free access to the garbage room, to empty his apartment.

After a week, a return visit was done, which resulted in the tenant losing his apartment. Instead of emptying his apartment of rubbish, he had put sheets over the piles. "What cannot be seen does not exist!" The tenant has never removed his rubbish since moving in a few years earlier. Instead, they had been stored in the dorm. When the landlord visited the approximately 10 square meter room, the piles were one meter high. The bottom bags had composted themselves. In addition to removing worms, flies, soil, and the smell, the tenant also moved out.

Unfortunately, it didn't go any better than that. We sat at another meeting a month later, and I, who came in a little late, wondered where the chairman was. "But haven't you heard! That person had the same problem!"

Nostalgia Saver – A person who, for sentimental reasons, cannot or does not want to get rid of things. It is common when one inherits a deceased relative and is forced to deal with the death cleaning.

The person operates by their emotions. There can be happy childhood memories in everything from photo albums to furniture. Memories that create the feeling of security. It makes it difficult to separate from movable things, such as ornaments and furniture, and fixed objects, such as their parents' house. Instead, one's own home gets filled to the point of becoming a hard-to-reach furniture store. Or instead of selling the parent's house, they choose to sell their own house and move "home" again for reasons that are not practical and long-term good, for example, being closer to work.

I remember a fellow student. When the last parent died, the apartment had to be emptied. The solution was most unexpected, at least for me. The deceased had only moved to a big city in his older years. However, my companion, the deceased's child, remembered the town of his childhood (if I remember correctly) and bought a house there. He moved all the deceased's belongings from the apartment to the newly purchased home, except the clothes that were given or thrown away.

The unexpected thing was that my friend did not move in himself, nor did he rent out the furnished house. Instead, he visited the house once a quarter to use the laundry room! The one-way journey was around four hours. Perhaps it was intended as an investment for the future.

Time to Plan When the Decluttering Will Take Place

Are There Vermin?

If the home has problems with vermin, such as bedbugs, clothes moths, wood-gnawing insects, and cockroaches, the reason they are there needs to be dealt with first. Addressing the apparent problem and killing the visible insect is insufficient. There are usually more vermin hiding.

Some cleaning measures or preventive measures you can do yourself. But certain vermin, such as bedbugs, in particular, require the help of a pest exterminator.

Bed bugs live and lay eggs in the darkest places of the room. If you have bed bugs, they live, for example, in or under your bed, sofa, and armchair, in wall sockets, behind skirting boards, and among clothes.

Bedbugs need to be treated in the home where they live. And for the best treatment, people need to sleep in the home during the treatment period. Different treatment methods depend on how big the problem has become for the tenant. In simpler cases, it is enough for the pest exterminator to put poison in the places where the bed bugs will pass over to get to their feeding place, i.e., the sleeping man. In case of a severe infestation in a defined area, for example, an apartment, the home can be heat treated. This means raising the temperature in the home to at least 55 degrees Celsius.

The most common advice on how to save clothes and textiles from bedbugs is as follows: Clothes and textiles can usually be "cleaned" by being washed and tumble-dried or dried at least 60 degrees Celsius for at least 1 hour. Textiles that cannot withstand the high temperatures can be packed in smaller bags and frozen at minus eighteen degrees Celsius. If it is a bag of approximately 1.5 kg, it must be kept frozen for at least three days. (Nomor, 2024)[1]

Do this in collaboration with the pest exterminator to synchronize the work effort. I have seen tenants who hoped that if they just heated and frozen their textiles, the problem would be solved. If you find bedbugs or other vermin in your clothes, they also live in other parts of your home.

Bringing bed bugs home from a trip or a friend's apartment is not embarrassing. It gets embarrassing the longer time goes by because the bed bugs not only ruin your night's sleep but can also start to spread to your nearest neighbors.

Get help as soon as you realize you have a pest problem.

Only when the pest exterminator clears a home and the homeowner no longer sees signs of bed bugs can a decluttering be planned. This prevents the bed bugs from spreading to someone else's home. (This also applies to other vermin.)

If you have had problems with bedbugs, cockroaches, wood-gnawing insects, or clothes moths, I wish, as your fellow man, that you would instead send furniture and clothes for recycling. Only if it is a genuine antique and you know that the furniture or clothes have been appropriately treated are worth passing on to a new owner.

Do you have a problem with **ants**? It would be best if you found their entrance. Once you know it, kill all the ants you see inside your home. Please put them in a garbage bag and throw it away immediately. Wet wipe the floor and the ants' walkways from the ants' entrance to other rooms or to and up cupboards and walls. The ants leave behind a scent that helps the rest of the family find their way.

The most common way to kill ants is to use ant poison. Preferably, it is placed outside where you see them entering and at the ants' entrance indoors. If there is a risk of pets and children getting access to the spread of poison, there is a reason to choose an alternative poison. My best tip is to check the grocery store's concentrated juice shelf. Look at the list of ingredients for the concentrated juices. If you find the content "aspartame," you have found the right product. Pour the concentrated juice into a jar lid and place the lid right at the ants' entrance indoors. If you can know the ants' entrance from the outside, treat that as well. Either with filled can lids or by pouring out the concentrated juice.

Do you have a problem with **mice**? I live in the country and always get some hibernating mice visiting every year in the walls or the attic. There are many different mouse traps, and I may not have tried them all. Or it's because the area I live in has a mutation of Einstein mice.

The best way I have found is to slice up a piece of carrot, poke a hole in the middle with a toothpick, and thread a thread through. Tie up the thread in a regular decent mousetrap. Make sure the safety pin is as straight as possible. In this way, the mouse will help pull the fuse and get stuck in the trap.

Picture 2. Mousetrap prepared with a piece of carrot.

Should You Declutter Yourself or Get Help From Someone?

The answer depends on your situation. You can probably handle the project if the home has few items. The more things there are to handle, the more people are needed. Ask family and friends or hire helpful people.

If heavier furniture is to be removed, having several people to help is more manageable. In that case, ensure which days people can help. Hiring a moving company may be the best solution if expensive furniture is to be moved. Make sure they have insurance and good references from previous clients.

If several people are involved, you must agree on the procedure before starting.

Hired people must primarily help you to be your hands and feet. You try to stay in the room as much as possible to decide and sort out things that you want to save, throw away, give away, and so on. To be able to give clear guidelines to those who help you.

Consider whether you need to schedule a babysitter or hire a dog sitter to maximize your time for your task.

Helping someone else

If you try to help another person, you first must ensure that the individual is involved in the decluttering project. Depending on the background of the problem, you two may have to start on your own for the first two to three days. So you can ensure that the person you are helping is with you 100 percent. The person himself must be involved. You must, of course, help, but primarily be a supervisor. Supervisor in the form of helping the person by asking the right questions and helping the person make decisions about each matter. See the upcoming chapter "How to Do It in Practical Terms."

Decide Which Two Weeks

Now is the time to take out the calendar to decide and book which two weeks suit you best.

By deciding the start and end days, you have created a goal for yourself. Based on that, you can choose to create milestones. For example, you can divide the rooms or objects (see below) on different days. Or follow the order mentioned in the next chapter, do as much as you can each day, and continue where you left off yesterday the next day. But to best ensure you stick to the plan, try dividing your rooms into specific days. Then, you can quickly see if you are behind and need to catch up. Also, try to leave one day per weekend free for other activities.

If you live in a house with a lot of storage in the basement and attic, schedule specific days to go through them. It must happen before adding new things.

Other areas that may need their own planned days, depending on their size and content, are the garage, workshop, outdoor storage, outdoor furniture, and garden. Remember that even objects such as extra houses on the real estate, mobile homes, caravans, boats, and rented warehouses may need to be decluttered. Plan them separately.

Preparatory Purchase

Make sure you have the following at home, or you will need to purchase it:

- Bucket and dust cloth. Any cleaning agent. You can go a long way with water, with or without a few drops of detergent. What you give away or want to sell needs to be clean. If you empty drawers and shelves, clean them before you put the things back. You can clean the other surfaces in the apartment or house if you have time or another day.

• Large plastic bags and smaller garbage bags.

• Pen to write on the boxes. Label the boxes with what they contain and where they are going.

• Pen to write on the plastic bags. Label the bags with what they contain and where they are going.

• Cardboard boxes—no bigger than you can carry yourself. Also, choose smaller boxes if you have books that you want to remove because books are heavy. The alternative is to fill larger boxes only to half.

• When you're out shopping, consider buying a new toilet brush, dish brush, dish cloth, and toothbrush (or toothbrush heads if you have an electric toothbrush). These things need to be replaced regularly but are usually deprioritized or forgotten.

• Steel wire for secure picture hanging of pictures. Check beforehand how much you need and whether you need to buy a new attachment solution.

• This is a reminder if you need and haven't yet bought mouse traps (and possibly wire and carrots) or poison for ants.

• Be prepared with something to eat and drink.

Booking Preparations

Finishing as soon as possible is always fun, but you're not meant to rush. Then, the risk is that it will be a less pleasant memory. It is better to break it down into smaller, manageable steps. In addition, things to be delivered to secondhand or recycling need to be adapted to the recipient's opening hours.

- If you do not have a washing machine in your home, the laundry needs to be booked.

- If dry cleaning is needed, leave everything when you've gone through the whole house. If it is a lot, perhaps for financial reasons, you want to split it up and take the most important first.

- If you need help taking things away to secondhand or recycling/garbage disposal, book a suitable day after you have finished your decluttering.

- If you have a car, make sure it has enough fuel. You do this to save time. Remember that trailers and heavier weights mean that all vehicles use more fuel. This also applies if you have an electric car. Expect the car to travel a shorter distance than usual. If you have had a diesel or petrol car before, your electric vehicle may be unable to pull the same weight. Also, ensure that you comply with the applicable regulations.

- If it's big things or so much that you need to borrow, rent a van, or rent a trailer, you need to schedule a day and time after you finish decluttering and know how much and where you must drive to use the vehicle time efficiently.

• If many things must be thrown away, you should check the best financial option for transporting them. You could rent a garbage container if you have room to put them on the plot. You could also use "big bags." If you are a tenant, talk to your landlord, who may already have proposals for a financial solution.

Picture 3. Garbage containers are a solution if you have space outside.

Rules of Conduct

Your goal is to declutter your home or another object in two weeks. You have already decided which weeks. Now, you must determine when you will perform this task each day. After this, you need to create a focused and productive environment.

Put music or the radio on if you want sound in the background. Do not watch TV until you're done. TV programs and news easily distract you. Turn off notifications from social media. If possible, put the phone away and turn off the cell phone ringer. (This may not work if you have a babysitter or dog sitter.) Otherwise, try only to check the phone during lunch and dinner breaks.

Prepare what you want to eat for breakfast, lunch, and dinner. The food should be prepared at home, so you only need to heat it. If you need help from relatives and friends, you must agree whether you will buy pizza or other fast food. Be prepared with something to drink.

Prepare a pitcher of water or water bottles to have drinking water nearby.

Choose comfortable and functional clothes that can get dirty. Assume it is a physical task, and you will likely get sweaty.

In What Order?

In What Order Do You Handle a Room?

Start by opening curtains and pulling up blinds to provide the best possible working light. In addition to ensuring good work lighting, you will appreciate fresh air from an open window, especially if your project is in a well-filled and untidy room.

It would be best to deal with each item once, starting with everything on the **floor**. By cleaning up the floor first, you'll have a better working environment as you tackle the rest of the room.

After the floor, you go through **things lying or standing** on tables, chests of drawers, speakers, cupboards, or other furniture.

After that, you tackle things hanging from the **ceiling**.

Then, what hangs on the **walls**?

Now, it's time to go through all the **open shelves**.

Next, go through every drawer, cupboard, wardrobe, or other **storage** option.

If possible and you see a need, wipe the shelves inside the cupboards and the drawers before placing or putting back contents. Since you have more rooms to go through, I suggest you wait to vacuum, mop the floors, and wipe the furniture until you have had time to go through your entire home. It is a premium that you can do later. The important thing now is to reduce the number of things so that cleaning takes less time.

In What Order Do You Take Different Rooms?

In crowded homes or estate

In overcrowded homes or estates, one can think a little differently. Start with the entrance and the hall until the nearest toilet. Then, choose to take one room at a time from the entrance. If you need a more preferred route, decide to go clockwise or counterclockwise from the front door. When the entrance floor is ready, then take the next floor.

If it's hot during the day, choose to deal with the wind in the morning. If it's hot in the afternoon, choose a room in the basement.

In normal cases

Start with the **bedroom** or sleeping corner/nook. It would be best to have a quiet and clean place to sleep. Falling asleep and waking up in a calm and decluttered environment provides better sleep and a better start to the day.

The same applies to the **children's room**. If the child is between three and eight years old, perhaps they can start thinking about whether there are things they want to give away. Or things that are broken that they want to throw away.

If the children are older, they can clean and declutter their rooms. If there are teenagers, they should be involved in cleaning and decluttering the rest of the home. So they learn for the future.

You know your children best, but if they have put things in the "Throw away" or "Give away" boxes, storing them for a few months might be wise. Afterward, you and your child go through the box together to ensure that the things in it can get thrown or given away.

Then aim at your **entrance hall**—the area, corridor, or room inside your front door. This surface will help you feel welcome at home. Having the season's shoes and outerwear on hand would be best. If you have a hat shelf or clothes hanger, the clothes you currently use should hang there. The rest are stored in a closet.

Many consider the **kitchen** to be the heart of the home. Cooking there should be fun. It would be best to have a clean workspace and functional relief surfaces here.

The **dining area** can be part of the kitchen or an adjoining room. Ensure your table surface is clear of anything other than what makes you happy or what you use while eating. Maybe a canvas, flowers in a vase, or candlesticks, but otherwise empty to accommodate the food you serve yourself, your family, or your friends.

The **toilet, shower**, and **bathroom** are the most visited places. These spaces need to be easy to clean because, unfortunately, they need to be cleaned more often than other rooms to remain pleasant.

There may be separate wardrobes or walk-in closets if the home does not have wardrobes in bedrooms or hallways. Clothes that hang or lie airy feel best, smell freshly washed, and have a longer lifespan.

The **living room** is usually the second meeting place in the home after the kitchen and dining area. The seating must be inviting, and the coffee table should be as empty as possible. If you have visitors, you want to be able to set out something to drink and maybe eat without first digging up the surface of the coffee table or moving the pile of freshly washed clothes from the armchair.

If there is a **balcony** or **patio**, it is there to be used. In addition to tables, chairs, cushion storage, possibly a carpet, and pots of vegetation, it should be relatively empty. Maybe a storage for the children's toys.

If you have a **laundry room**, this is the next area to get organized. There needs to be relief areas and hanging possibilities here. If your washing machine, drying cabinet, and tumble dryer are in the bathroom, you are already done with this one.

If you have other types of rooms, now is the time to take them. For example, you may have a **study** or a **guest room**. Ensure order in these rooms/areas as well. Here, you should be creative and have/get energy when you tinker and work.

For those of you who live in a house, some of the above spaces can be found in the **basement**. The basement is usually the number one storage place for things stored seasonally or long-term. Going through and sorting out stuff you don't want to keep anymore may need a scheduled day, depending on how much you have.

It is essential that you can reach the shut-off valves for incoming water, gas, electricity, and district heating.

If there is a floor drain, storage on shelves is recommended, as extreme weather can make the street's sewer lines unable to swallow all the water. If sewage or storm water seeps up through your floor drain, you would appreciate it afterward if you had stored your most valuable items off the floor or on the top shelf closest to the ceiling. However, remember that the air must be able to circulate in the basement and along the basement walls.

The **attic** can be the second storage place for seasonal or long-term items for homeowners. Your goal should be to know where things are and be able to reach them easily.

The construction of the attic and the roof's maintenance needs can affect whether moisture will damage your items if stored in it. Remember not to store flammable substances that can spontaneously ignite at high temperatures. The attic should not be overcrowded with things that prevent the air from circulating.

Other areas that may need planned days, depending on their size and content, are **garages** and **workshops**, **outdoor** storage, outdoor furniture, and **gardens**. Other objects, such as **extra houses** on the real estate or somewhere else, **mobile homes, caravans, boats,** and **rented warehouses,** may also need their planned days.

36

What Can Be Cleared Away?

Image 4. The best way to find something is to clean the house.

Books – Keep the books you remember being good, the ones that make you happy, or books you want to read or save for some reason. Books you don't want to read can be given away or sold.

When it comes to older nonfiction books on specific topics that you think you "might" be interested in reading and using, it's good to remember that there are likely newer nonfiction books with updated information and knowledge. If, on the other hand, it is "old subjects" that are close to your heart, that type of book may no longer be available for purchase.

Clothes – Be honest with yourself. Think about which garments you use. Delicate dresses or party clothes may not be used often, but they are good to keep if you can imagine using them again. Or if they have great emotional value and make you happy. Otherwise, you can give away anything you have not used in the last two years. Or what you don't want to use in the coming year. There will likely be someone else who will want to use the garment instead of you. Torn clothes are thrown away (unless they were "fashionably tattered" from the beginning).

Electronic equipment and machinery – You can give away things that work but are no longer used. If they don't start and lack value, throw them away.

Older equipment and machinery can be valuable to any hobbyist who likes to fix broken things. You can always advertise or search for ads if you have the time.

Furniture and paintings – If reasonably intact, reselling them to new owners is often possible. If they are of little value, the quickest way is to donate them to secondhand.

Groceries – Review the pantry, spice cabinet, fridge, and freezer. Clear out everything that has passed the best-before date. In the pantry and refrigerator, "look-smell-taste" applies to decide whether it can stay. If you don't want to smell or taste it now, you don't want to do it next month either. It is just as well to throw it away now instead of in a few months or years. If you want to take the "cautious" route, discard if the best-before date in the pantry, spice cabinet, and freezer has passed by a year.

Have you frozen something that you don't know what it is? Throw it away. Throw away everything you don't feel like cooking or eating in the next week (if you have the time and desire to do so).

A garbage bag filled with fresh and frozen goods is thrown into the garbage collection as soon as possible.

Hobbies and interests – If you have a particular area of interest that you collect, it's good to think about how you store them. Make sure that it is you who lives and decides in your home and not your collectibles. Removing old and broken things makes room for new stuff you can and need to use. Consider what it says if any of the areas in this chapter are one of your interests.

Kitchen appliances – Do you find kitchen appliances purchased and used intensively initially but have since been left standing? Check if they still work, clean them, and give them away.

Ornaments/Small items – Give them away if they don't make you happy or evoke positive memories. If a grandchild or friend in the future admires the fine thing and perhaps expresses the desire to own one, test the idea of giving it away. If it feels good, give it away.

Plants – If you have too many healthy plants, consider giving some away. Throw away dead and withered plants. Keep pots that you like. If you couldn't care for the plants you had, choose simpler plants or those that better fit your lifestyle. If you need to replant flowers, plan a separate day for that.

Simpler plants are, for example, orchids. Orchids only need one shot glass (3 cl) of water a week. If you have forgotten it or are going away for a long time, let the plant stand in water for 20-30 minutes. It will feel good again and survive well for at least a month if not placed in direct sunlight.

If you have plants in the bedroom, remember that they produce oxygen during the day but carbon dioxide in the evening. If possible, open a window when you sleep, especially if the bedroom does not have an excellent mechanical air supply.

Porcelain, glass, cutlery, and kitchen utensils – Broken things should be thrown away unless there is an extremely good reason to keep them. Try putting broken but still-want-to-keep stuff in a storage box you will check in a few months. Is it still necessary to keep it? If you needed the thing, you probably already picked it up.

If you have several sets of crockery, consider whether you shouldn't start using your fine crockery and give away the everyday ones. You deserve to eat and drink with the fine set every day. You don't have to wait for a more friendly dinner party.

Shoes – Throw away worn-out or torn shoes or shoes where the rubber or plastic has hardened or cracked. The likelihood that your feet would feel good walking in them again is minimal. Newer shoes you don't use for any reason and are still in good condition are sent to secondhand stores.

How To Do It in Practical Terms?

Image 5. Decluttering is the art of making space for the things that truly matter.

Finally, it is time to start with the most fun but challenging part: deciding what to keep and what to get rid of.

There are certain things that you know immediately when you look at them that you want to keep. But far from all things are so simple. If you don't know immediately, take the object in your hands. If there are larger objects, put your hand/hands on them.

What is the immediate thought, memory, or feeling comes to mind? If the object gives you **positive** thoughts, memories, or emotions, it can be kept (if you want to).

If **negative** thoughts, memories, and feelings appear, I advise you to eliminate the object.

If the item is complete and functional but more or less **neutral** to you, ask yourself the following questions: Do I need this item? Has it been used in the last year? Will it be used in the coming year?

Some objects, such as photo albums or fine clothes, may have sentimental value. They may be used less often but have value in themselves to remain in your possessions. Or maybe there is someone you have in mind who you can ask if they want the item.

Do I Need This Item?

The most important question you will learn to ask yourself during your decluttering is: **Do I need this item?**

Doing this practical exercise when you go to the shops would be best. You learn to think twice before buying things in the future. So that you buy what you know you need and know you will use. Instead of buying something just because it's nice or fun to have. Or because everyone else has one. Or you've seen an advertisement for the product.

Because you don't want another decluttering in a few years again, do you? It is more fun to save and invest money so that it earns interest so you can buy a new sofa or go on a holiday trip. Or a down payment for a new home, car, or retirement (OK, that last one didn't sound so fun).

Things You Want to Keep

Decide which **things you need** or wish to keep inside the home. For practical reasons, store what is often used close at hand.

The next question is where to place the items that should remain in the home. Where do you want to store similar items? Do they have a place in a cupboard, drawer, or wardrobe? Things that make you happy are used daily or continuously; you can, for example, leave them on the kitchen counter or a chest of drawers.

Then, immediately put what you have to store in the home in the right place.

Chemicals must be kept somewhere children or pets cannot reach them.

Set up boxes and plastic bags for the "Stored" category for **long-term storage** so that items can be quickly put inside.

Things to be stored long-term in boxes are stored in the storage area you hopefully already have in connection with your home. Larger things that are used less often but do not fit in the storage room (or for other practical reasons cannot be stored in the storage room) may need to be stored in the home. Think about all the possibilities that exist. If, for example, your skis bring you positive memories and a happy mind, then why not place them as an ornament securely attached to the wall? They help motivate you when you save money for your next ski trip. (You may need to check with your landlord to see if the solution is OK before implementing wild solutions.)

Before renting a storage room to store things, consider whether it's worth it. Ensure your home storage options contain only things you want to store because they will be used one day. The more storage options you have, the greater the risk that they will be filled with stuff instead of you getting rid of things all at once.

Things You Don't Want to Keep

You can **sell** items in good condition if you find it fun and have the time. Otherwise, they will be added to your collection for **giveaways**.

You may have borrowed things from someone. Try **returning** them. Otherwise, you give them away if the owner says it's OK.

If you have help from someone who you notice is interested in something you have, ask if the person wants to borrow it. Many people think it is easier to "borrow" than to "get." **Lending things out** means you may be able to borrow them back later, but assume that you're effectively giving them away.

Broken things and rubbish you **throw away**. You may need to sort rubbish into different fractions depending on where you live and which regulations apply.

There may be recycling requirements for packaging such as glass, paper, plastic, metal, electronics, batteries, lamps, PET bottles, aluminum cans, and wood waste. Chemicals, compostable, burnable, furniture, textiles, landfills, etc. If you don't already know, check what applies in your area.

On the evening of the last day, what is to be stored long-term should have been moved to the right place. Items you want to eliminate may not have left your home due to impracticality (if it's the weekend). But in that case, you have boxes and bags containing things to ship away. If you haven't already planned which day the removal will take place, now is the time to decide. Now you know exactly how much you have and where to go. Or it would be best if you found out who to contact to pick things up.

Conclusion

Most people have a knack for collecting something special. The reason for the gathering can vary greatly. It's OK as long as things don't take over the person's life or home.

Before you help someone else, it is good to have made your decluttering journey yourself. When you help someone else, it is essential to be patient and understanding because thoughts or feelings usually cause the gathering in the first place. But most people are happy to get help decluttering. Gratitude may only be expressed afterward.

In the case of a large collector, it is necessary to prepare and think a little differently. Or if it concerns a death cleaning after a relative.

Without a decided start and stop schedule, the likelihood that your decluttering project will turn into a halfhearted attempt or never be finished increases. So, use the calendar and look for good opportunities. Ask the people involved and decide the date to start decluttering.

I hope you, who have read this far, realize you can complete your decluttering. It works, and it is possible. It is only up to you to decide to implement it.

In addition to a quieter home that you enjoy being in and a calmer mind, I hope you learned the financial importance of stopping in the store and asking yourself: **Do I need this item?**

Remember to keep things that bring you positive thoughts, memories, or feelings. Store things that you use regularly close at hand in the home. Things used less often can be stored in storage rooms or closets.

I hope this book will help you to declutter your home. I would appreciate it if you left a positive review on Amazon and let me know how it went.

Take care, and remember to take one thing at a time!

Remember! When you're done with your decluttering journey and no longer need this book, pass it on to someone in need.

With pure love,

Mari Sellin

Make a Difference with Your Review

UNLOCK THE POWER OF GENEROSITY

"Alone, we can do so little; together, we can do so much."

- HELEN KELLER

Imagine being the spark that encourages someone to finally bring order to their life! Your experience could be the gentle nudge someone else needs to take the first step from chaos to a calm, organized space.

From Chaos to Order isn't just a book; it's a guide, a companion, and a toolkit for those ready to transform their space and mindset. And by sharing your thoughts, you'll help others decide if this book can be their guide, too.

Why Leave a Review?

Every review helps readers discover what's possible with a bit of guidance and motivation. Your review could be that "aha" moment for someone just starting their journey. In just a few words, you could help...

...one more person finds peace in a once-cluttered space.

...one more family creates order and harmony in their home.

...one more busy professional regains focus and control.

...one more dreamer creates a life of purpose and calm.

Ready to make an impact?

If you enjoyed the book, please consider leaving a review on the site where you purchased it. You can help transform someone's journey from chaos to order in less than a minute.

If helping others is your thing, thank you for sharing your experience. I'm grateful for every single review.

Thank you from the bottom of my heart!

Mari Sellin

References and Attributions

Image References

Images created with the assistance of OpenAI's DALL-E and retouched by Mari Sellin are:

Cover – Bedroom

Image 1 - A living room

Image 2 – Kitchen table

Image 3 – Room

Image 4 – Bookshelf

Image 5 – Oil painting of bedroom table

Photographic Attributions

The photographs were created by:

Picture 1 – Eurasian Dog Elise with a motorcycle by Ulf Gardelin

Picture 2 – Mousetrap by Mari Sellin

Picture 3 – Garbage Containers by Mari Sellin

About the Author

Mari Sellin is a renowned property consultant in Sweden with a rich background in helping property owners manage, develop, and optimize their properties from financial and technical perspectives. With extensive experience in project management and operational efficiency, Mari has become a trusted advisor in the property industry.

Previously, Mari dedicated her efforts to assisting individuals in decluttering their homes and providing much-needed support to those in need. Today, she primarily focuses on helping companies streamline their operations, enhancing productivity and effectiveness.

Mari, an entrepreneur, educator, and author, believes in every individual's untapped potential. She is passionate about helping people achieve more by offering the proper support and direction.

Mari is also the founder of Admiranda Publishing (Admiranda Förlag AB), a Swedish company committed to publishing insightful and practical books.

https://www.facebook.com/AdmirandaPublishing

Also by Mari Sellin

"**Weekend Decluttering** – From Chaos to Calm in 48 Hours for Home Harmony and Inner Peace"

A concise guide designed for smaller homes with up to three rooms and a kitchen.

"A Practical Guide to Real Estate Investing for Beginners - Simple Strategies to Grasp the Market, Invest Wisely, and Manage Money & Risks for Long-Term Wealth for You and Your Family"

Unlock the potential of real estate investing with practical tools and strategies for creating wealth and security for your family.

[1] *Vägglus - bekämpning och sanering av vägglöss - Nomor.* (n.d.). https://nomor.se/se/fakta-rad/skadedjur/vaggloss/

Don't miss out!

Visit the website below and you can sign up to receive emails whenever Mari Sellin publishes a new book. There's no charge and no obligation.

https://books2read.com/r/B-A-BTBYC-NIUJF

Connecting independent readers to independent writers.

Also by Mari Sellin

From Chaos to Order - 14 Days of Advanced Decluttering

About the Author

Mari, an entrepreneur, educator, and author, believes in each individual's untapped potential. She's driven by her passion for helping people achieve more and offering the support and guidance they need to thrive.

Mari Sellin is a civil engineer with a degree from the Royal Institute of Technology and a seasoned real estate consultant known for her expertise in helping property owners maximize their assets' financial and technical potential. With a knack for project management and a talent for boosting operational efficiency, she's become a go-to advisor in the property industry.

In addition to her career, Mari founded Admiranda Publishing, an independent publishing house created to give a voice to her stories and those of other talented authors. Admiranda Publishing specializes in bringing to life fiction and non-fiction works that inspire, educate, and entertain readers everywhere. Find more information about Admiranda Publishing on Facebook.

www.ingramcontent.com/pod-product-compliance
Lightning Source LLC
Chambersburg PA
CBHW070556160726

48003CB00005B/2076